LET'S EXPLORE EUROPE!

European Union

You can find this booklet and other short, clear explanations about the EU online at
europa.eu.int/comm/publications

European Commission
Directorate-General for Press and Communication
Publications
B-1049 Brussels

Manuscript finalised in May 2005

Cover illustration and interior photos of the children: Reporters

The European Commission wishes to thank the staff and pupils of the European School,
Woluwe (Belgium), for their contributions to this publication.

Luxembourg: Office for Official Publications of the European Communities, 2005

ISBN 92-894-8390-3
44 pp. – 21 x 29.7 cm
© European Communities, 2005
Reproduction is authorised.

Printed in Germany

PRINTED ON WHITE CHLORINE-FREE PAPER

LET'S EXPLORE EUROPE!

Hello! Welcome to Europe – our home.

It's a beautiful place and there's lots happening here.
How much do you know about it?

Come with us and let's explore Europe together! It will be an adventure journey through time and space and you'll find out loads of interesting things.

As we go along, test yourself to see how much you've learnt. Go to our website europa.eu.int/europago/explore/ and try the quiz about each chapter.

You can also have fun doing games and activities on the 'Europa Go' website europa.eu.int/europago/welcome.jsp

Ready? Then let's begin!

What's in this book?

A continent to discover

Europe is one of the world's seven continents. The others are Africa, America, Antarctica, Asia, Australia and Oceania.

Europe stretches all the way from the Arctic in the north to the Mediterranean Sea in the south, and from the Atlantic Ocean in the west to Asia in the east. It has many rivers, lakes and mountain ranges. The map (page 4) tells you the names of some of the biggest ones.

The highest mountain in Europe is Mount Elbrus, in the Caucasus mountains, on the border between Russia and Georgia. Its highest peak is 5 642 metres above sea level.

The highest mountain in western Europe is Mont Blanc, in the Alps, on the border between France and Italy. Its summit is over 4 800 metres above sea level.

Mount Elbrus, the highest mountain in Europe.

Also in the Alps is Lake Geneva – the largest freshwater lake in western Europe. It lies between France and Switzerland, goes as deep as 310 metres and holds about 89 trillion litres of water.

Lake Geneva, in the Alps.

The largest lake in central Europe is Balaton, in Hungary. It is 77 kilometres (km) long and covers an area of about 600 square kilometres (km^2). Northern Europe has even bigger lakes, including Saimaa in Finland (1 147 km^2) and Vänern in Sweden (more than 5 500 km^2).

Lake Saimaa, in Finland.

The continent of Europe

Pelicans on the Danube delta, Romania.

One of Europe's longest rivers is the Danube. It rises in the Black Forest region and flows eastwards through 10 countries (Germany, Austria, Slovakia, Hungary, Croatia, Serbia, Bulgaria, Romania, Moldova and Ukraine) to Romania, where it forms a delta on the Black Sea coast. In all, it covers a distance of about 2 850 km.

Other big rivers include the Rhine (about 1 320 km long), the Elbe (about 1 170 km) and the Loire (more than 1 000 km). Can you find them on the map?

The Loire valley is famous for its beautiful castles.

Big rivers are very useful for transporting things. All kinds of goods are loaded onto barges that carry them up and down the rivers, between Europe's sea ports and cities far inland.

A cargo barge travels up the Rhine.

Getting around

For getting around Europe, roads and railways are even more useful than rivers.

The first railway engine – Stephenson's 'Rocket'.

Did you know that railways were invented in Europe? George Stephenson introduced the first passenger train in 1825. It was called 'the Rocket' and it reached a speed of 25 kilometres per hour (km/h) – which was really fast for those days.

Today, Europe's high-speed electric trains are very different from those first steam engines. They are very comfortable and they travel at speeds of up to 330 km/h on specially built tracks. More tracks are being built all the time, to allow people to travel as quickly as possible between Europe's big cities.

Roads and railways sometimes have to cross mountain ranges, wide rivers or even the sea. So engineers have built some very long bridges and tunnels. The longest road tunnel in Europe is the Laerdal tunnel in Norway, between Bergen and Oslo. It is more than 24 kilometres (km) long and was opened in November 2000.

The longest railway tunnel in Europe is the Channel Tunnel. It carries Eurostar high-speed trains under the sea between Calais in France and Folkestone in England, and it's more than 50 km long.

Eurostar trains at Waterloo station (London).

The highest bridge in the world (245 metres tall) is the Millau Viaduct in France, which was opened in December 2004.

Two of the longest bridges in Europe are the Oresund road and rail bridge (16 km long) between Denmark and Sweden and the Vasco da Gama road bridge (more than 17 km long) across the river Tagus in Portugal. The Vasco da Gama bridge is named after a famous explorer, and you can read about him in the chapter 'A journey through time'.

The world's highest bridge – the Millau Viaduct (France).

People also travel around Europe by plane, because air travel is quick. Some of the world's best planes are built in Europe – for example, the Airbus. Different European countries make different parts of an Airbus, and then a team of engineers puts the whole plane together. The biggest passenger plane in the world is the Airbus A380, designed to carry up to 840 passengers. It first flew in April 2005.

The world's biggest passenger plane – the Airbus A380.

The fastest ever passenger plane, the Concorde, was designed by a team of French and British engineers. Concorde could fly at 2 160 km/h – twice the speed of sound – and could cross the Atlantic in less than three hours! (Most planes take about eight hours).

Faster than any plane are space rockets, such as Ariane – a joint project between several European countries. People don't travel in the Ariane rocket: it is used to launch satellites, which are needed for TV and mobile phone networks, for scientific research and so on. Most of the world's satellites are now launched using these European rockets.

The Ariane 5 rocket puts satellites into space.

The success of Concorde, Airbus and Ariane show what can be achieved when European countries work together.

Climate and nature

Most of Europe has a 'temperate' climate – neither too hot nor too cold. The coldest places are in the far north and in the high mountains, where winter night temperatures can be as low as -40 °C. The warmest places are in the far south and south-east, where summer daytime temperatures can be as high as + 40 °C.

The weather is warmest and driest in summer (roughly June to September) and coldest in winter (roughly December to March). However, Europe's weather is very changeable, and in many places it can rain at almost any time of year.

Coping with the winter

Wild animals in cold regions usually have thick fur or feathers to keep them warm, and their coats may be white to camouflage them in the snow. Some spend the winter sleeping to save energy. This is called *hibernating*.

The Arctic fox ...

... and snowy owl are well camouflaged.

The marmot ...

... and European brown bears live in the mountains, where they spend the winter sleeping.

Many species of birds live on insects, small water creatures or other food that cannot easily be found during cold winter months. So they fly south in the autumn and don't return until spring. Some travel thousands of kilometres, across the Mediterranean Sea and the Sahara Desert, to spend the winter in Africa. This seasonal travelling is called *migrating*.

Swallows ...

... and even flamingos come to Europe in spring.

Enjoying the spring and summer

When spring comes to Europe (March to May), the weather gets warmer. Snow and ice melt. Baby fish and insect larvae swarm in the streams and ponds. Migrating birds return to make their nests and raise their families. Flowers open, and bees carry pollen from one plant to another.

Trees put out new leaves which catch the sunlight and use its energy to make the tree grow. In mountain regions, farmers move their cows up into the high meadows, where there is now plenty of fresh grass.

Summer is good in the mountain meadow.

Lizards love warm weather.

Cold-blooded animals such as reptiles also need the sun to give them energy. In summer, especially in southern Europe, you will often see lizards basking in the sunshine and hear the chirping of grasshoppers and cicadas.

Autumn: a time of change

In late summer and autumn, the days grow shorter and the nights cooler. Many delicious fruits ripen at this time of year, and farmers are kept busy harvesting them. Nuts too ripen in autumn, and squirrels will gather and store heaps of them ready for the winter.

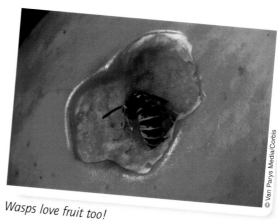

Wasps love fruit too!

Squirrels store nuts for their winter food.

Many trees shed their leaves in autumn because there is no longer enough sunshine for the leaves to be useful. They gradually change from green to shades of yellow, red, gold and brown. Then they fall, carpeting the ground with colour. The fallen leaves decay, enriching the soil and providing food for future generations of plant life.

This yearly cycle of the seasons, and the changes it brings, make the European countryside what it is – beautiful, and very varied.

Autumn carpets the woods with colour.

Farming

On high mountains and in the far north of Europe, farming is impossible because it is too cold for crops to grow. But evergreen trees such as pines and firs can survive cold winters. That is why Europe's coldest places are covered with evergreen forests. People use the wood from these forests to make many things – from houses and furniture to paper and cardboard packaging.

Wooden houses in Bergen, Norway.

Further south, most of the land is good for farming. It produces a wide variety of crops including wheat, maize, sugar beet, potatoes and all sorts of fruit and vegetables.

Oranges are grown in warm countries like Spain and are good for our health as they are full of vitamin C.

Harvesting grapes in the Czech Republic.

Where there is plenty of sunshine and hardly any frost (near the Mediterranean, for example), farmers can grow fruit such as oranges and lemons, grapes and olives. Olives contain oil which can be squeezed out of the fruit and used in preparing food. Grapes are squeezed to get the juice, which can be turned into wine. Europe is famous for its very good wines, which are sold all over the world.

These grapes will be made into red wine.

11

© Van Parys Media/Corbis

Crops in dry regions need irrigating.

Mediterranean farmers also grow lots of other fruit and vegetables. Tomatoes, for example, ripen well in the southern sunshine. But vegetables need plenty of water, so farmers in hot, dry regions will often have to irrigate their crops. That means giving them water from rivers or from under the ground.

Grass grows easily where there is enough rain, even if the soil is shallow or not very fertile. Many European farmers keep animals that eat grass – such as cows, sheep or goats. They provide milk, meat and other useful products like wool and leather.

© Van Parys Media/Corbis

Sheep grazing on grasslands in Spain.

© Van Parys Media/Corbis

Pigs can be kept indoors.

Many farmers also keep pigs or chickens. These animals can be raised almost anywhere because they can be kept indoors and given specially prepared feed. Chickens provide not only meat but eggs too, and some farms produce thousands of eggs every day.

© Zefa

Chickens provide eggs, which contain lots of protein and help us stay healthy.

Farms in Europe range from very big to very small. Some have large fields – which makes it easy to harvest crops using big machines. Others, for example in hilly areas, may have small fields. Walls or hedgerows between fields help stop the wind and rain from carrying away soil, and they can be good for wildlife too.

A patchwork of fields in Europe.

The countryside is for everyone to enjoy.

Many city people like to spend weekends and holidays in the European countryside, enjoying the scenery, the peace and quiet and the fresh air. We all need to do what we can to look after the countryside and keep it beautiful.

The sea

Europe has thousands and thousands of kilometres of beautiful coastline, which nature has shaped in various ways. There are tall rocky cliffs, and beautiful beaches of sand or colourful pebbles formed by the sea as it pounds away at the rocks, century after century.

The sea shaped these chalk cliffs.

A glacier carved this fjord.

In Norway, glaciers have carved the coast into steep-sided valleys called fjords. In some other countries, the sea and wind pile up the sand into dunes. The highest dune in Europe (117 metres tall) is the Dune du Pyla, near Arcachon in France.

The Pyla sand dune - Europe's tallest.

One of Europe's rarest animals – the monk seal – lives in the Mediterranean.

Many kinds of fish and other animals live in the sea around Europe's coasts. They provide food for seabirds, and for marine mammals such as seals. Where rivers flow into the sea, flocks of waders come to feed, at low tide, on creatures that live in the mud.

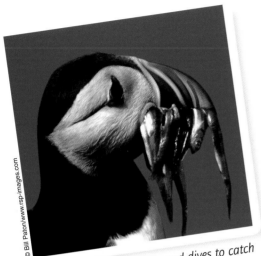

The puffin nests on cliffs, and dives to catch fish.

Flocks of waders find food in river estuaries.

People and the sea

The sea is important for people too. The Mediterranean was so important to the Romans that they called it *Mare nostrum*: 'our sea'. Down through the centuries, Europeans have sailed the world's oceans, discovered the other continents, explored them, traded with them and made their homes there. In the chapter 'A journey through time' you can find out more about these great voyages of discovery.

Cargo boats from around the world bring all kinds of goods (often packed in containers) to Europe's busy ports. Here they are unloaded onto trains, lorries and barges. Then the ships load up with things that have been produced here and which are going to be sold on other continents.

Container ships carry goods to and from Europe.

Some of the world's finest ships have been built in Europe. They include Queen Mary 2 – the world's biggest ever passenger liner. She made her first transatlantic voyage in January 2004.

The world's biggest passenger ship – Queen Mary 2.

© Andrew Ross

© Van Parys Media/Corbis

Scuba diving on the coast of Malta.

Europe's seaside resorts are great places for a holiday. You can enjoy all kinds of water sports, from surfing and boating to waterskiing and scuba diving. Or you can just relax – sunbathing on the beach and cooling off in the sea.

Fishing

Fishing has always been important for people in Europe. Whole towns have grown up around fishing harbours, and thousands of people earn their living by catching and selling fish or doing things for the fishermen and their families.

© Van Parys Media/Corbis

Europeans eat many kinds of fish. Tuna is one of the biggest!

© Reporters

A modern factory trawler in Rotterdam (Netherlands).

Modern fishing boats, such as factory trawlers, can catch huge numbers of fish. To make sure that enough are left in the sea, European countries have agreed rules about how many fish can be caught, and about using nets that let young fish escape.

Another way to make sure we have enough fish is to farm them. On the coasts of northern Europe, salmon are reared in large cages in the sea. Shellfish such as mussels, oysters and clams can be farmed in the same way.

You don't always need a boat to go fishing!

Farming salmon in Scotland.

Protecting Europe's coasts

Europe's coasts and the sea are important to wildlife and to people. So we need to look after them. We have to prevent them becoming polluted by waste from factories and towns. Oil tankers sometimes have accidents, spilling huge amounts of oil into the sea. This can turn beaches black and kill thousands of seabirds.

European countries are working together to try to prevent these things from happening and to make sure that our coastline will remain beautiful for future generations to enjoy.

Portugal – on the western edge of Europe.

A journey through time

Over thousands of years, Europe has changed enormously.
It's a fascinating story! But it's a long one, so here are just some of
the highlights.

The Stone Age

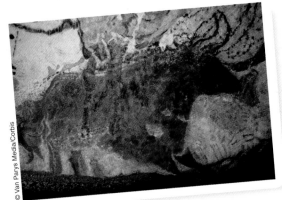

The earliest Europeans were hunters and lived in caves. On the walls of some caves they made wonderful paintings of hunting scenes. Eventually, they learnt farming and began breeding animals, growing crops and living in villages.

Prehistoric cave paintings at Lascaux, France.

They made their weapons and tools from stone – by sharpening pieces of flint, for example.

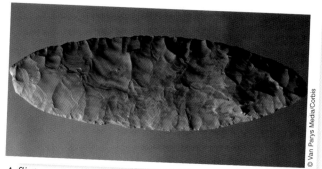

A flint weapon from the Stone Age.

Learning to use metal – the Bronze and Iron Ages

Several thousand years BC (before the birth of Christ), people discovered how to get different metals by heating different kinds of rock in a very hot fire. Bronze – a mixture of copper and tin – was hard enough for making tools and weapons. Gold and silver were soft but very beautiful and could be shaped into ornaments.

A bronze axe head.

Later, an even harder metal was discovered: iron. The best kind of iron was steel, which was strong and didn't easily break, so it made good swords. But making steel was very tricky, so good swords were rare and valuable!

Ancient Greece – roughly 2000 to 200 BC

In Greece about 4 000 years ago, people began to build cities. At first they were ruled by kings. Later, around 500 BC, the city of Athens introduced 'democracy' – which means 'government by the people.' (Instead of having a king, the men of Athens took decisions by voting). Democracy is an important European invention that has spread around the world.

An ancient Greek temple still standing today (in Athens).

Some of the other things the ancient Greeks gave us include:

- wonderful stories about gods and heroes, wars and adventures;
- elegant temples, marble statues and beautiful pottery;
- the Olympic Games;
- well-designed theatres, and great writers whose plays are still performed today;
- teachers like Socrates and Plato, who taught people how to think logically;
- mathematicians like Euclid and Pythagoras, who worked out the patterns and rules in maths;
- scientists like Aristotle (who studied plants and animals) and Eratosthenes (who proved that the earth is a sphere and worked out how big it is).

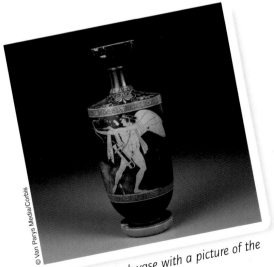

An ancient Greek vase with a picture of the god Eros.

Plato, one of the world's great thinkers.

The Roman Empire – roughly 500 BC to 500 AD
(AD means after the birth of Christ)

Rome started out as just a city in Italy. But the Romans were very well organised, their army was very good at fighting and they gradually conquered all the lands around the Mediterranean. Eventually the Roman Empire stretched all the way from northern England to the Sahara Desert and from the Atlantic to Asia.

Part of ancient Rome – and what the Roman soldiers looked like.

Here are some of the things the Romans gave us:

- good, straight roads connecting all parts of the empire;
- beautiful houses with courtyards and mosaic tiled floors;
- strong bridges and aqueducts (for carrying water long distances);
- round-topped arches – which made their buildings solid and long-lasting;
- new building materials, such as cement and concrete;
- new weapons such as catapults;
- important laws, which many European countries still use today;
- the Latin language;
- great writers like Cicero and Virgil.

A Roman mosaic showing a mythical character.

A Roman aqueduct still standing today: the Pont du Gard in France.

The Middle Ages – roughly 500 to 1500 AD

When the Roman Empire collapsed, different parts of Europe were taken over by different tribes. For example...

The Celts. Their descendants today live mainly in Brittany (France), Cornwall (England), Galicia (Spain), Ireland, Scotland and Wales. In these parts of Europe, Celtic languages and culture are very much alive.

Celtic art from about the 700s AD.

The Vikings were such good sailors they even reached America (but didn't tell anyone!).

The Germanic peoples. Not all of them settled in Germany:

- **The Angles and Saxons** moved to England and ruled it until 1066.
- **The Franks** conquered a large part of Europe, including France, between about 500 and 800 AD. Their most famous king was Charlemagne.
- **The Goths** (*Visigoths* and *Ostrogoths*) set up kingdoms in Spain and Italy.
- **The Vikings** lived in Scandinavia. In the 800s and 900s AD they sailed to other countries, stealing treasure, trading and settling where there was good farmland.

The Normans, or 'Northmen', were Vikings who settled in France (in the area we call Normandy) and then conquered England in 1066. A famous Norman tapestry shows scenes from this conquest. It is kept in a museum in the town of Bayeux.

A battle scene from the Bayeux tapestry.

The Slavs settled in many parts of eastern Europe and became the ancestors of today's Slavic-speaking peoples, including Belorussians, Bulgarians, Croatians, Czechs, Poles, Russians, Serbs, Slovaks, Slovenes and Ukrainians.

The Magyars settled in eastern Europe and founded the Kingdom of Hungary in the 900s AD. Their descendants today live in Hungary and other neighbouring countries.

During the Middle Ages, kings and nobles in Europe often quarrelled and there were many wars. (This was the time when knights in armour fought on horseback). To defend themselves from attack, kings and nobles often lived in strong castles, with thick stone walls. Some castles were so strong they have lasted until today.

Medieval castles were built to keep out enemies.

Christianity became the main religion in Europe during the Middle Ages, and churches were built almost everywhere. Some of them are very impressive – especially the great cathedrals, with their tall towers and colourful stained-glass windows.

'Gothic' architecture (such as in Chartres cathedral, France) was a great invention of the Middle Ages.

In southern Spain, where Islam was the main religion, the rulers built beautiful mosques and minarets. The most famous ones left today are the mosque in Cordoba and the Giralda minaret in Seville.

Part of the huge medieval mosque in Cordoba (Spain).

The Renaissance – roughly 1300 to 1600 AD

During the Middle Ages, most people could not read or write and they knew only what they learnt in church. Only a few clever teachers in universities had copies of the books the ancient Greeks and Romans had written. But in the 1300s and 1400s, students began rediscovering the ancient books. They were amazed at the great ideas and knowledge they found there, and the news began to spread.

Wealthy and educated people, for example in Florence (Italy), became very interested. They could afford to buy books – especially once printing was invented in Europe (1445) – and they fell in love with ancient Greece and Rome. They had their homes modelled on Roman palaces, and they paid talented artists and sculptors to decorate them with scenes from Greek and Roman stories, and with statues of gods, heroes and emperors.

One of the world's most famous statues: David by Michelangelo.

It was as if a lost world of beauty and wisdom had been reborn. That is why we call this period the 'Renaissance' (meaning 'rebirth'). It gave the world:

- great painters and sculptors such as Michelangelo and Botticelli;
- talented architects like Brunelleschi;
- the amazing inventor and artist Leonardo da Vinci;
- great thinkers such as Thomas More, Erasmus and Montaigne;
- scientists such as Copernicus and Galileo (who discovered that the earth and other planets move around the sun);
- beautiful buildings such as the castles in the Loire valley;
- a new interest in what human beings can achieve.

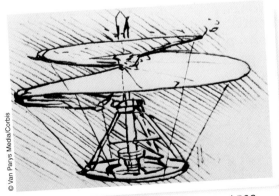

Leonardo da Vinci designed this 'helicopter' 500 years ago!

One of the great Renaissance paintings: Venus by Botticelli.

Great discoveries and new ideas – roughly 1500 to 1900 AD

At the time of the Renaissance, trade with distant lands was becoming very important for European merchants. For example, they were selling goods in India and bringing back valuable spices and precious stones. But travelling overland was difficult and took a long time, so the merchants wanted to reach India by sea. The problem was, Africa was in the way – and it is very big!

However, if the world really was round (as people were beginning to believe), European ships ought to be able to reach India by sailing west. So, in 1492, Christopher Columbus and his sailors set out from Spain and crossed the Atlantic. But instead of reaching India they discovered the Bahamas (islands in the Caribbean Sea, near the coast of America).

Replicas of Christopher Columbus's ships.

Vasco da Gama – the first man to sail from Europe to India.

Other explorers soon followed. In 1497-98, Vasco da Gama – a Portuguese naval officer – was the first European to reach India by sailing around Africa. In 1519-1522, another Portuguese explorer – Ferdinand Magellan – became the first person to sail right round the world!

The dodo, a flightless bird, once lived on an island in the Indian Ocean. It was driven to extinction by European colonists.

Before long, Europeans were exploring the Caribbean islands and America (which they called the 'new world') and founding colonies there. In other words, they took over the land, claiming it now belonged to their home country in Europe. They took their beliefs, customs and languages with them – and that is how English and French came to be the main languages spoken in North America, and Spanish and Portuguese in Central and South America.

As time passed, Europeans sailed further and further – to China, Japan, South-East Asia, Australia and Oceania. Sailors returning from these distant lands reported seeing strange creatures very different from those in Europe. This made scientists keen to explore these places and to bring back animals and plants for Europe's museums. In the 1800s, European explorers went deep into Africa and by 1910 European nations had colonised the whole African continent.

Meanwhile, back in Europe, scientists were finding out more and more about about how the universe works. Geologists, studying rocks and fossils, began wondering how the earth had been formed and how old it really was. Two great scientists, Jean-Baptiste Lamarck and Charles Darwin, eventually concluded that animals and plants had 'evolved' – changing from one species into another over millions and millions of years.

Charles Darwin published his theory of evolution in 1859.

Voltaire, one of the great writers of the Enlightenment age.

In the 1700s, people were asking other important questions too – such as how countries should be governed, and what rights and freedoms people should have. The French writer Jean-Jacques Rousseau said that everyone should be equal. Another French writer, Voltaire, said the world would be better if reason and knowledge replaced ignorance and superstition.

This age of new ideas, called the 'Enlightenment', led to revolutions in some countries – for example the French revolution of 1789, when the king and queen and many of the nobles were beheaded.

The Industrial Revolution – roughly 1750 to 1880 AD

A different kind of 'revolution' started in Europe about 250 years ago – in the world of 'industry'. It all began with an energy crisis. For thousands of years, people had been burning wood and charcoal. But now, parts of Europe were running out of forests! What else could we use as fuel?

Henry Bessemer – inventor of modern steelmaking.

The answer was coal. There was plenty of it in Europe, and miners began digging for it. Coal powered the newly-invented steam engines. It could also be roasted and turned into 'coke', which is a much cleaner fuel – ideal for making iron and steel.

About 150 years ago, a man called Henry Bessemer invented a 'blast furnace' that could produce large amounts of steel quite cheaply. Soon Europe was producing huge quantities of it, and it changed the world! Cheap steel made it possible to build skyscrapers, huge bridges, ocean liners, cars, fridges... Powerful guns and bombs too.

The modern world – roughly 1880 until today

Other European inventions from the 1870s onwards helped create the world we know today.
For example:

The telephone	1875	Television and motorways	1920s
The petrol engine	1886	Radar and the biro pen	1935
First radio messages	1901	Instant coffee	1937
Bakelite, the first plastic	1909	First jet aircraft	1939
Neon lighting	1912	First computer	1940s

Today, roughly a quarter of the people working in Europe are producing things needed for the modern world: food and drinks; mobile phones and computers; clothes and furniture; washing machines and televisions; cars, buses and lorries and lots more besides.

About seven out of every 10 European workers have 'service' jobs. In other words, they work in shops and post offices, banks and insurance companies, hotels and restaurants, hospitals and schools, etc. – either selling things or providing services that people need.

The first telephone – invented by Scottish-born Alexander Graham Bell. Today, Europe makes the latest mobile phones.

Learning the lessons of history

Sadly, the story of Europe is not all about great achievements we can be proud of. There are also many things to be ashamed of. Down the centuries, European nations fought terrible wars against each other. These wars were usually about power and property, or religion.

European colonists killed millions of native people on other continents – by fighting or mistreating them, or by accidentally spreading European diseases among them. Europeans also took millions of Africans to work as slaves.

A war cemetery in Flanders (Belgium). More than eight million soldiers died in the First World War alone.

Lessons had to be learnt from these dreadful wrong-doings. The European slave trade was abolished in the 1800s. Colonies gained their freedom in the 1900s. And peace did come to Europe at last.
To find out how, read the chapter called 'Bringing the family together : the story of the European Union'.

Forty famous faces, A to Z

Many of the world's great artists, composers, entertainers, inventors, scientists and sports people have come from Europe. We mentioned some of them in earlier chapters. We can't possibly include them all in this book, so here are just 40 more names, in alphabetical order and from various European countries, with photos of some of them.

We have left a blank space on page 29 for your own personal choice. It could be someone famous from your own country, or your favourite European sports team or pop group. Why not find a picture of them and stick it into the blank space, along with a few facts about them?

Name	Nationality	What they did
Abba	Swedish	Pop group: their songs were big hits around the world in the 1970s.
Štefan Banič	Slovakian	Inventor: he invented the parachute in 1913.
The Beatles	British	Pop group: their songs were big hits around the world in the 1960s.
Henri Becquerel	French	Scientist: he discovered radioactivity in 1896.
Ludwig van Beethoven	German	Composer: wrote a lot of great music. *The Ode to Joy* (the European anthem) comes from his ninth symphony.
Tim Berners-Lee	British	Inventor: he invented the World Wide Web, on which the Internet is based.
Niels Bohr	Danish	Scientist: won the Nobel Prize for Physics in 1922, for his discoveries about the structure of atoms.
Robert Boyle	Irish	Scientist: famous for his experiments on gases and the discovery of 'Boyle's Law'.
Charlie Chaplin	British	Film director and one of the world's funniest actors. His great films include *Modern times*.
Fryderyk Chopin	Polish	Composer and pianist: he wrote many piano pieces including his famous *Preludes*.
Nadia Comaneci	Romanian	Athlete: the first person ever to score full marks (10 out of 10) for gymnastics in the Olympic Games, in 1976.
Marie Curie (Maria Sklodowska)	Polish	Scientist: with her husband Pierre she discovered radium – a radioactive metal. They were awarded the Nobel Prize for Physics in 1903.
Salvador Dalí	Spanish	Artist: famous for his strange, dreamlike paintings in the 'surrealist' style.

Tim Berners-Lee

Nadia Comaneci

Marie Curie

Name	Nationality	What they did
Marlene Dietrich	German	Actress: she starred in many films, including the original version of *Around the world in 80 days.*
Antonin Dvorak	Czech	Composer: his great pieces include the *New World Symphony.*
Albert Einstein	German	Scientist: he discovered 'relativity' – in other words, how matter, energy and time are all related to one another.
Federico Fellini	Italian	Film director: his great films, including *La Strada*, won him five Oscar awards.
Milos Forman	Czech	Film director: he won Oscars for his films *Amadeus* and *One Flew Over the Cuckoo's Nest.*
Sigmund Freud	Austrian	Psychiatrist: he developed 'psychoanalysis' – a way of explaining how our minds work.
Justine Henin-Hardenne	Belgian	Tennis player: she won a gold medal at the 2004 Olympic Games.
Hergé (Georges Rémi)	Belgian	Artist and writer: he created the *Tintin* adventures and many other comic book series
Heinrich Hertz	German	Scientist: in 1888 he proved that radio waves exist.
Georges-Henri Lemaître	Belgian	Scientist: in 1933 he put forward the 'Big Bang' theory, explaining how the universe began.
Franz Liszt	Hungarian	Composer: he wrote some of the world's most difficult piano music, such as the *Transcendental Studies.*
Claude Monet	French	Artist: famous for his 'impressionist' style paintings, including several series of *Water-lilies.*
Wolfgang Amadeus Mozart	Austrian	Composer: he wrote a lot of great music, including the opera *The Magic Flute.*
Isaac Newton	British	Scientist: in the 1600s he discovered how gravity works, and how the planets move through space.

Marlene Dietrich

Albert Einstein

Federico Fellini

Justine Henin-Hardenne

Franz Liszt

Name	Nationality	What they did
Alfred Nobel	Swedish	Scientist: he invented dynamite in 1866, and he founded the Nobel Prize for great achievements.
Erkki Nool	Estonian	Athlete: he won a gold medal in the decathlon at the 2000 Olympic Games.
Louis Pasteur	French	Scientist: he discovered that many diseases are caused by germs, and in 1862 he invented 'pasteurisation', a way of killing germs in food.
Pablo Picasso	Spanish	Artist: famous for his paintings in the 'cubist' style, including *Les demoiselles d'Avignon*.
Marco Polo	Croatian Venetian	Great explorer: more than 700 years ago he travelled through Asia to China, and back again.
Rembrandt	Dutch	Artist: famous for his use of rich colour, light and shadow. His paintings include *The Night Watch*.
Michael Schumacher	German	Racing driver: he won the World Championship for several years running.
Jean Sibelius	Finnish	Composer: his great pieces include *Finlandia*.
U2	Irish	Rock band: their songs have been big hits around the world since 1980.
Vincent Van Gogh	Dutch	Artist: his many paintings include several of *Sunflowers*.
Antonio Vivaldi	Italian	Composer: he wrote many pieces, including *The Four Seasons*.
Alessandro Volta	Italian	Scientist: around 1799 he invented the electric battery.
Zinedine Zidane	French	Footballer: officially the best player of the year in 1998 and 2000.
ONE MORE: MY CHOICE		

Pablo Picasso

U2

Zinedine Zidane

My choice:

Languages in Europe

People in Europe speak many different languages. Most of these
languages belong to three large groups or 'families': Germanic, Slavic
and Romance. The languages in each group share a family likeness because they are descended from
the same ancestors. For example, Romance languages are descended from Latin – the language spoken
by the Romans.

Here's how to say 'Good morning' or 'Hello' in just a few of these languages.

Germanic

Danish	*God morgen*
Dutch	*Goedemorgen*
English	*Good morning*
German	*Guten Morgen*
Swedish	*God morgon*

Romance

French	*Bonjour*
Italian	*Buon giorno*
Portuguese	*Bom dia*
Spanish	*Buenos días*

Slavic

Czech	*Dobre rano*
Polish	*Dzień dobry*
Slovak	*Dobré ráno*
Slovene	*Dobro jutro*

It's not hard to see the family likeness in these examples. But there are other European languages
that are less closely related, or not at all related, to one another.
Here's how to say 'Good morning' or 'Hello' in just a dozen of these languages.

Basque	*Egun on*	Hungarian	*Jó reggelt*
Breton	*Demat*	Irish	*Dia dhuit*
Estonian	*Tere hommikust*	Latvian	*Labrīt*
Finnish	*Hyvää huomenta*	Lithuanian	*Labas Rytas*
Gaelic (Scottish)	*Madainn mhath*	Maltese	*L-Ghodwa t-Tajba*
Greek	*Kalimera*	Welsh	*Bore da*

In the language of the Roma people, who live in many parts of Europe, 'Good morning' is *Lasho dyes*.

Learning languages can be great fun – and it's important on a continent like ours. Many of us enjoy
going on holiday to other European countries, and getting to know the people there. That's a great
opportunity to practise the phrases we know in different languages.

A family of peoples

We Europeans belong to many different countries, with different languages, traditions, customs and beliefs. Yet we belong together, like a big family, for all sorts of reasons. Here are some of them.

- We have shared this continent for thousands of years.
- Our languages are often related to one another.
- Many people in every country are descended from people from other countries.
- Our traditions, customs and festivals often have the same origins.
- We share and enjoy the beautiful music and art, and the many plays and stories, that people from all over Europe have given us, down the centuries.
- Almost everyone in Europe believes in things like fair play, neighbourliness, freedom to have your own opinions, respect for each other and caring for people in need.

So we enjoy what's different and special about our own country and region, but we also enjoy what we have in common as Europeans.

War and peace

Sadly, there have been many quarrels in the European family. Often they were about who should rule a country, or which country owned which piece of land. Sometimes a ruler wanted to gain more power by conquering his neighbours.

© Van Parys Media/Corbis

Europe in 1945.

One way or another, for hundreds of years, there were terrible wars in Europe. In the 20th century, two big wars started on this continent but spread and involved countries all around the world. That is why they are called World Wars. They killed millions of people and left Europe poor and in ruins.

Could anything be done to stop these things happening again? Would Europeans ever learn to sit down together and discuss things instead of fighting? The answer is yes. That's the story of our next chapter: the story of the European Union.

Bringing the family together: the story of the European Union

The Second World War ended in 1945. It had been a time of terrible destruction and killing, and it had started in Europe. How could the leaders of European countries stop such dreadful things from ever happening again? They needed a really good plan that had never been tried before.

A brand new idea

Jean Monnet

A Frenchman called Jean Monnet thought hard about this. He realised that there were two things a country needed before it could make war: iron for producing steel (to make tanks, guns, bombs and so on) and coal to provide the energy for factories and railways. Europe had plenty of coal and steel: that's why European countries had easily been able to make weapons and go to war.

So Jean Monnet came up with a very daring new idea. His idea was that the governments of France and Germany – and perhaps of other European countries too – should no longer run their own coal and steel industries. Instead, these industries should be organised by people from all the countries involved, and they would sit around a table and discuss and decide things together. That way, war between them would be impossible!

Jean Monnet felt that his plan really would work if only European leaders were willing to try it. He spoke about it to his friend Robert Schuman, who was a minister in the French government. Robert Schuman thought it was a brilliant idea, and he announced it in an important speech on 9 May 1950.

Robert Schuman

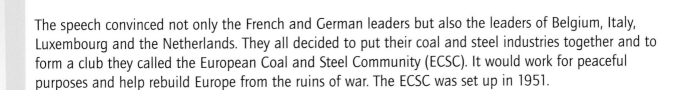

The speech convinced not only the French and German leaders but also the leaders of Belgium, Italy, Luxembourg and the Netherlands. They all decided to put their coal and steel industries together and to form a club they called the European Coal and Steel Community (ECSC). It would work for peaceful purposes and help rebuild Europe from the ruins of war. The ECSC was set up in 1951.

The common market

The six countries got on so well working together that they soon decided to start another club, called the European Economic Community (EEC). It was set up in 1957.

'Economic' means 'to do with the *economy*' – in other words, to do with money, business, jobs and trade.

Bored at the border... Queues like this used to be part of normal life in Europe.

One of the main ideas was that the EEC countries would share a 'common market', to make it easier to trade together. Until then, lorries and trains and barges carrying goods from one country to another always had to stop at the border, and papers had to be checked and money called 'customs duties' had to be paid. This held things up and made goods from abroad more expensive.

The point of having a common market was to get rid of all those border checks and delays and customs duties, and to allow countries to trade with one another just as if they were all one single country.

Food and farming

The Second World War had made it very difficult for Europe to produce food or to import it from other continents. Europe was short of food even in the early 1950s. So the EEC decided on an arrangement for paying its farmers to produce more food, and to make sure that they could earn a decent living from the land.

This arrangement was called the 'common agricultural policy' (or CAP). It worked well. So well, in fact, that farmers ended up producing *too much* food, and the arrangement had to be changed! Nowadays, the CAP pays farmers mostly to look after the countryside.

Machines like this combine harvester are used to harvest wheat and other crops.

From EEC to European Union

The common market was soon making life easier for people in the EEC. They had more money to spend, more food to eat and more varied things in their shops. Other neighbouring countries saw this and, in the 1960s, some of them began asking whether they too could join the club. After years of discussions, Britain, Denmark and Ireland joined in 1973. It was the turn of Greece in 1981, followed by Portugal and Spain in 1986, Austria, Finland and Sweden in 1995. So now the club had 15 members.

Joining the club. In this picture, Denmark signs up for membership.

Protecting the environment includes reducing air pollution – for example, using wind energy to make electricity.

Over these years, the club was changing. By the end of 1992 it had finished building the 'single market' (as it became known), and it was doing a lot more besides. For example, EEC countries were working together to protect the environment and to build better roads and railways right across Europe. Richer countries helped poorer ones with their road-building and other important projects.

To make life easier for travellers, most EEC countries had got rid of passport checks at the borders between them. A person living in one member country was free to go and live and find work in any other member country. The governments were discussing other new ideas too – for example, how policemen from different countries could help one another catch criminals, drug smugglers and terrorists.

A policeman and his dog check luggage for drugs.

In short, the club was so different and so much more united that, in 1992, it decided to change its name to the 'European Union' (EU).

Bringing the family together

Meanwhile, exciting things were happening beyond the EU's borders. For many years, the eastern and western parts of Europe had been kept apart. They weren't at war, but their leaders disagreed strongly. The rulers of the eastern part believed in a system of government called 'Communism' which did not allow people much freedom. Because of the way they were governed, those countries were poor compared to western Europe.

The division between east and west was so strong it was often described as an 'iron curtain'. In many places the border was marked by tall fences or a high wall, like the one that ran through the city of Berlin and split Germany in two. It was very difficult to get permission to cross this border.

Finally, in 1989, the division and disagreement ended. The Berlin Wall was knocked down and the 'iron curtain' ceased to exist. Soon, Germany was reunited. The peoples of the eastern part of Europe chose for themselves new governments that got rid of the old, strict Communist system. They were free at last! It was a wonderful time of celebration.

1989: demolishing the Berlin Wall.

The countries that had gained freedom began asking whether they could join the European Union, and soon there was quite a queue of 'candidate' countries waiting to become EU members.

Before a country can join the European Union, its economy has to be working well. It also has to be democratic – in other words, its people must be free to choose who they want to govern them. And it must respect human rights. (Human rights include the right to say what you think, the right not to be put in prison without a fair trial, the right not to be tortured, and many other important rights as well).

The candidate countries worked hard at all these things and, after a few years, 10 of them were ready. They joined the EU on 1 May 2004. They are Cyprus, the Czech Republic, Estonia, Hungary, Latvia, Lithuania, Malta, Poland, Slovakia and Slovenia.

1 May 2004: celebrating a great day.

Never before had so many countries joined the EU at the same time, so this was a very special occasion. People were particularly happy because this was a real 'family reunion', bringing together at last the eastern and western parts of Europe.

What the EU does

The EU tries to make life better in all sorts of ways. Here are some of them.

The environment

The environment belongs to everyone, so countries have to work together to protect it. The EU has rules about stopping pollution and about protecting, for example, wild birds. These rules apply in all EU countries and their governments have to make sure those rules are obeyed.

Pollution crosses borders, so EU countries work together to protect the environment.

Jobs

It's important for people to have jobs that they enjoy and are good at. Some of the money they earn goes to pay for hospitals and schools, and to look after old people. That's why the EU is doing all it can to create new and better jobs for everyone who can work. It helps people to set up new businesses, and provides money to train people to do new kinds of work.

Training people to do new jobs is very important.

Freedom!

People living in the EU are free to live, work or study in whichever EU country they choose, and the EU is doing all it can to make it simple to move home from one country to another. When you cross the borders between most EU countries, you no longer need a passport. The EU encourages students and young people to spend some time studying or training in another European country.

Students from different countries study together, with help from the EU.

The euro

In years gone by, each country in Europe had its own kind of money, or 'currency'. Now there is one single currency, the euro, which all EU countries can share if they wish. Having one currency makes it easier to do business and to travel and shop all over the EU without having to change from one currency to another.

It took nine years of hard work and careful planning to introduce the euro. The notes and coins came into use on 1 January 2002. The euro has replaced the old currencies in 12 of the EU's member countries. The others are not using it yet. If you compare euro coins you will see that on one side there is a design representing the country it was made in. The other side is the same for all the countries

The euro is used in many EU countries.

Helping regions in difficulty

Life is not easy for everyone everywhere in Europe. In some places there are not enough jobs for people, because mines or factories have closed down. In some areas, farming is hard because of the climate, or trade is difficult because there are not enough roads and railways.

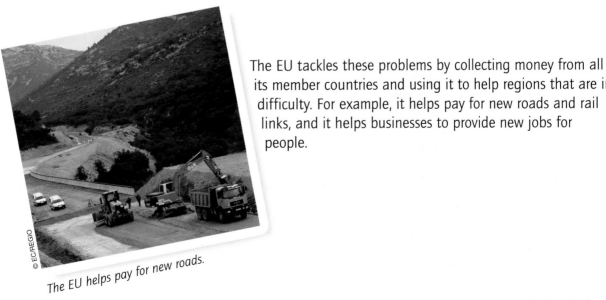

The EU tackles these problems by collecting money from all its member countries and using it to help regions that are in difficulty. For example, it helps pay for new roads and rail links, and it helps businesses to provide new jobs for people.

The EU helps pay for new roads.

Helping poor countries

In many countries around the world, people are dying or living difficult lives because of war, disease and natural disasters such as droughts or floods. Often these countries do not have enough money to build the schools and hospitals, roads and houses that their people need.

The EU gives money to these countries, and sends teachers, doctors, engineers and other experts to work there. It also buys many things that those countries produce without charging customs duties. That way, the poor countries can earn more money.

The EU delivers food to people in need.

Peace

The European Union has brought many European countries together in friendship. They don't always agree on everything, but that's normal. (Do people in your family always agree on everything?) What is good is that the leaders of EU countries sit round a table to sort out their disagreements instead of fighting.

So the dream of Jean Monnet and Robert Schuman has come true: the EU has brought peace among its members. It is also working for lasting peace among its neighbours and in the wider world. For example, EU soldiers and police officers are helping keep the peace in the former Yugoslavia, where there was bitter fighting not many years ago.

These are just some of the things the EU does: there are many more. In fact, being in the European Union makes a difference to just about every aspect of our lives.

Europe has its own flag and its own anthem – the *Ode to Joy* from Beethoven's ninth symphony. The original words are in German, but when used as the European anthem it has no words – only the tune. You can hear it on the Internet:
europa.eu.int/abc/symbols/anthem/index_en.htm

The European flag.

The European Union and its neighbours

Key

The coloured countries are members of the European Union (EU).

The striped countries are planning to join the EU.

The other countries, including those shown by a small circle, are neighbours of the EU.

The dots show where the capital cities are.

Vatican City is in Rome.

Some islands and other pieces of land belonging to France, Portugal and Spain are part of the EU.

But they are a long way from mainland Europe, so we have put them in the box (top right).

The European Union countries

The countries are in alphabetical order according to what each country is called in its own language or languages (as shown in brackets).

Flag	Country	Capital City	Population
	Belgium (België; Belgique)	Brussels (Brussel; Bruxelles)	10.4 million
	Czech Republic (Česká republika)	Prague (Praha)	10.2 million
	Denmark (Danmark)	Copenhagen (København)	5.4 million
	Germany (Deutschland)	Berlin (Berlin)	82.5 million
	Estonia (Eesti)	Tallinn (Tallinn)	1.4 million
	Greece (Ελλάαδ/Ellada)	Athens (Αθήνα/Athinai)	11.0 million
	Spain (España)	Madrid (Madrid)	40.7 million
	France (France)	Paris (Paris)	59.6 million
	Ireland (Ireland; Eire)	Dublin (Dublin; Baile Atha Cliath)	4.0 million
	Italy (Italia)	Rome (Roma)	57.3 million
	Cyprus (Κύπρος/Kypros) (Kibris)	Nicosia (Λευκωσία/Lefkosia) (Lefkosa)	0.7 million
	Latvia (Latvija)	Riga (Riga)	2.3 million
	Lithuania (Lietuva)	Vilnius (Vilnius)	3.5 million

Flag	Country	Capital City	Population
	Luxembourg (Luxembourg)	Luxembourg (Luxembourg)	0.5 million
	Hungary (Magyarország)	Budapest (Budapest)	10.1 million
	Malta (Malta)	Valletta (Valletta)	0.4 million
	Netherlands (Nederland)	Amsterdam (Amsterdam)	16.2 million
	Austria (Österreich)	Vienna (Wien)	8.1 million
	Poland (Polska)	Warsaw (Warszawa)	38.2 million
	Portugal (Portugal)	Lisbon (Lisboa)	10.4 million
	Slovenia (Slovenija)	Ljubljana (Ljubljana)	2.0 million
	Slovakia (Slovensko)	Bratislava (Bratislava)	5.4 million
	Finland (Suomi; Finland)	Helsinki (Helsinki; Helsingfors)	5.2 million
	Sweden (Sverige)	Stockholm (Stockholm)	8.9 million
	United Kingdom (*) (United Kingdom)	London (London)	59.3 million

(*) The full name of this country is 'the United Kingdom of Great Britain and Northern Ireland', but for short most people just call it Britain, the United Kingdom or the UK.

Population figures are for 1 January 2004.
Source: *Eurostat.*

How the EU takes decisions

As you can imagine, it takes a lot of effort by a lot of people to organise the EU and make everything work. Who does what?

The European Commission

In Brussels, 25 women and men (one from each EU country) meet every Wednesday to discuss what needs to be done next. These people are called 'commissioners', and together they make up the European Commission. Their job is to think about what would be best for the EU as a whole, and to propose new laws for the EU as a whole. In their work they are helped by experts, lawyers, secretaries, translators and so on.

Once they have agreed what law to propose, they send their proposal to the European Parliament and the Council of the European Union.

Mr Barroso, from Portugal, is President of the European Commission until 2009.

The European Parliament

The European Parliament represents all the people in the EU. It holds a big meeting every month, in Strasbourg, to discuss the new laws being proposed by the European Commission. If the Parliament doesn't like a proposal, it can ask the Commission to change it until Parliament is satisfied that this is a good law.

There are 732 members of the European Parliament (MEPs). They are chosen, every five years, in an election when all the adult citizens of the EU get the chance to vote.

Mr Borrell Fontelles, from Spain, is President of the European Parliament until 2007.

The Council of the European Union

MEPs are not the only people who decide on new EU laws. They also have to be discussed by government ministers from all the EU countries. When the ministers meet together they are called 'the Council of the European Union'.

After discussing a proposal, the Council votes on it. There are rules about how many votes each country has, and how many are needed to pass a law. In some cases, the rule says the Council has to be in complete agreement.

Once the Council and the Parliament have passed a new law, EU governments have to make sure it is respected in their countries.

Ministers from all the EU governments meet to pass EU laws.

The Court of Justice

If a country doesn't apply the law properly, the European Commission will warn it, and may complain about it to the European Court of Justice, in Luxembourg. The Court's job is to make sure that EU laws are respected, and are applied in the same way everywhere. It has one judge from each EU country.

There are other groups of people (committees of experts and so on) involved in taking these decisions, because it's important to get them right. If you want to know more about these people and what they do, try reading the booklet *How the European Union works*, online at **europa.eu.int/comm/publications/booklets/ eu_glance/53/index_en.htm** It's meant for adults, but it's not very hard to read.

The Court makes sure everyone is treated equally under EU law.

Tomorrow... and beyond

There are big challenges facing the world right now. For example:

- How can we stop the pollution which is making the world's climate change?
- How can we protect the world's forests and other natural environments?
- How can we make life better for the world's poor and hungry people?
- How can we bring peace to the world's trouble-spots?
- How should we deal with terrorism?

The EU is tackling these problems, but it can't solve them on its own. It needs to work with other countries around the world. And, of course, its leaders need to agree together on what to do.

What would you like the EU to do about the world's big problems?
Do you have any good ideas for doing things better?
Why not discuss your ideas with your family, your friends and teachers...

We are today's European children: before long we'll be Europe's adults.
The future is for us to decide – together!

The future is in your hands...

© Van Parys Media/Corbis

2075

44

Other information on the European Union

 Information in all the official languages of the European Union is available on the Internet. You can access it through the Europa server: **europa.eu.int**

 All over Europe there are hundreds of local EU information centres. You can can find the address of the centre nearest you at this website: **europa.eu.int/comm/relays/index_en.htm**

 EUROPE DIRECT is a service which answers your questions about the European Union. You can contact this service by freephone: **00 800 6 7 8 9 10 11** (or by payphone from outside the EU: +32-2-299 96 96), or by electronic mail via europa.eu.int/europedirect

You can also obtain information and booklets in English about the European Union from:

EUROPEAN COMMISSION
REPRESENTATIONS

Representation in Ireland
18 Dawson Street
Dublin 2
Tel. (353-1) 634 11 11
Fax (353-1) 634 11 12
Internet: www.euireland.ie
E-mail: eu-ie-info-request@cec.eu.int

Representation in the United Kingdom
8 Storey's Gate
London SW1P 3AT
Tel. (44-20) 79 73 19 92
Fax (44-20) 79 73 19 00/10
Internet: www.cec.org.uk

Representation in Wales
2 Caspian Point, Caspian Way
Cardiff CF10 4QQ
Tel. (44-29) 20 89 50 20
Fax (44-29) 20 89 50 35
Internet: www.cec.org.uk

Representation in Scotland
9 Alva Street
Edinburgh EH2 4PH
Tel. (44-131) 225 20 58
Fax (44-131) 226 41 05
Internet: www.cec.org.uk

Representation in Northern Ireland
Windsor House
9/15 Bedford Street
Belfast BT2 7EG
Tel. (44-28) 90 24 07 08
Fax (44-28) 90 24 82 41
Internet: www.cec.org.uk

Information services in the United States
2300 M Street, NW - 3rd Floor
Washington DC 20037
Tel. (202) 862 95 00
Fax (202) 429 17 66
Internet: www.eurunion.org

222 East 41st Street, 20th Floor
New York, NY 10017
Tel. (212) 371 38 04
Fax (212) 688 10 13
Internet: www.eurunion.org

EUROPEAN PARLIAMENT
OFFICES

Office in Ireland
European Union House
43 Molesworth Street
Dublin 2
Tel. (353-1) 605 79 00
Fax (353-1) 605 79 99
Internet: www.europarl.ie
E-mail: epdublin@europarl.eu.int

United Kingdom Office
2 Queen Anne's Gate
London SW1H 9AA
Tel. (44-20) 72 27 43 00
Fax (44-20) 72 27 43 02
Internet: www.europarl.org.uk
E-mail: eplondon@europarl.eu.int

Office in Scotland
The Tun
4 Jackson's Entry
Holyrood Road
Edinburgh EH8 8PJ
Tel. (44-131) 557 78 66
Fax (44-131) 557 49 77
Internet: www.europarl.org.uk
E-mail: epedinburgh@europarl.eu.int

There are European Commission and Parliament representations and offices in all the countries of the European Union. The European Commission also has delegations in other parts of the world.

EN

Europe: a beautiful continent with a fascinating history. It has produced many of the world's famous scientists, inventors, artists and composers, as well as popular entertainers and successful sports people.

For centuries Europe was plagued by wars and divisions. But in the last 50 years or so, the countries of this old continent have at last been coming together in peace, friendship and unity, to work for a better Europe and a better world.

This book for children (roughly 9 to 12 years old) tells the story simply and clearly. Full of interesting facts and colourful illustrations, it gives a lively overview of Europe and explains briefly what the European Union is and how it works.

Each chapter links to an online quiz (**europa.eu.int/europago/explore/**), and there are games on the 'Europa Go' website (**europa.eu.int/europago/welcome.jsp**).

Have fun exploring!

NA-63-04-359-EN-C

ISBN 92-894-8390-3

9 789289 483902

Publications Office
Publications.eu.int